It's
Chinese New Year!

by Richard Sebra

BUMBA BOOKS™

LERNER PUBLICATIONS ◆ MINNEAPOLIS

3 2401 00901 484 8

Note to Educators:

Throughout this book, you'll find critical thinking questions. These can be used to engage young readers in thinking critically about the topic and in using the text and photos to do so.

Lerner Publications Company
A division of Lerner Publishing Group, Inc.
241 First Avenue North
Minneapolis, MN 55401 USA

For reading levels and more information, look up this title at www.lernerbooks.com.

Library of Congress Cataloging-in-Publication Data

Names: Sebra, Richard, 1984– author.
Title: It's Chinese New Year! / by Richard Sebra.
Description: Minneapolis : Lerner Publications, [2017] | Series: Bumba books—It's a holiday! | Includes bibliographical references and index.
Identifiers: LCCN 2015048783 (print) | LCCN 2016007009 (ebook) | ISBN 9781512414257 (lb : alk. paper) | ISBN 9781512414936 (pb : alk. paper) | ISBN 9781512414943 (eb pdf)
Subjects: LCSH: New Year—China—Juvenile literature. | China—Social life and customs—Juvenile literature.
Classification: LCC GT4905 .S38 2017 (print) | LCC GT4905 (ebook) | DDC 394.261—dc23

LC record available at http://lccn.loc.gov/2015048783

Manufactured in the United States of America
1 – VP – 7/15/16

LERNER
SOURCE™

Expand learning beyond the printed book. Download free, complementary educational resources for this book from our website, www.lerneresource.com.

Table of Contents

Chinese New Year

It is time to celebrate.

Chinese New Year

is here!

This holiday happens in

January or February.

Every year is named after an animal.

There are twelve different calendar animals.

The animal changes each year.

Why do you think the years have animal names?

A new year in China
means a new season.
Spring is coming.
Spring is a time to
see family.

People honor the gods they believe in.

They also remember loved ones who have died.

Some people light candles.

How else might you remember loved ones?

Families have big feasts.

People eat a lot of food.

Many people eat oranges too.

People decorate

with red.

This color means

good luck.

People dance to celebrate.

Some people dress as dragons.

Dragons are lucky in China.

Why do you think dragons are lucky?

Children get gifts.

Adults give them red envelopes.

Money is inside the envelopes.

Chinese New Year celebrates

the past.

Families come together.

They look forward to the new year.

Chinese Calendar

rat

pig

ox

dog

tiger

rooster

鼠 猪

牛 狗

虎 鸡

兔 猴

龙 羊

蛇 马

rabbit

monkey

dragon

goat

snake

horse

22

Picture Glossary

candles

wax sticks that can be burned for light

dragons

pretend animals with wings and tails

envelopes

paper containers for letters or money

feasts

large meals

Index

Read More

Heinrichs, Ann. *Chinese New Year*. Mankato, MN: The Child's World, 2013.

Pettiford, Rebecca. *Chinese New Year*. Minneapolis: Jump!, 2016.

Qaiser, Annie. *China*. Mankato, MN: The Child's World, 2015.

Photo Credits